POLICE DOGS
ON THE JOB

BY BRANDON TERRELL

The Child's World®
childsworld.com

Published by The Child's World®
1980 Lookout Drive • Mankato, MN 56003-1705
800-599-READ • www.childsworld.com

Photographs ©: Jason Hoekema/Valley Morning Star/AP Images, cover, 1; Peter Isotalo, 5; Luis Santana/iStockphoto, 6; Paul Valade/Daily Herald/ AP Images, 8; Chris Shipley/The Morning Call/AP Images, 9; Grisha Bruev/ Shutterstock Images, 10; Shutterstock Images, 12, 13; Kachalkina Veronika/ Shutterstock Images, 14; Lance Cpl. Thomas Mudd/U.S. Marine Corps, 15; Michael Pereckas CC2.0, 16; Kelly Nelson/Shutterstock Images, 17; iStockphoto, 18; John Roman Images/Shutterstock Images, 20

ISBN 9781503816145

LCCN 2016945655

Printed in the United States of America
PA02318

TABLE OF CONTENTS

FAST FACTS

The Job

- Police dogs have many jobs. They track **criminals** and find missing people. They also search buildings and sniff out **illegal** materials.
- When it is time for a police dog to **retire**, the dog lives the remainder of its life with its **handler**. The two have worked together for years and have created a lasting bond.

Training Time

- Police dogs must first learn **obedience**.
- The dogs must then complete ten weeks of police dog training.
- Once police dogs are on the job, training continues every day.

Common Breeds

- The first police dogs were German shepherds. They remain a common police dog breed.
- Another common police dog is the Belgian Malinois. It is similar to the German shepherd but smaller.
- Bloodhounds work as police dogs for detective and tracking work.

Famous Dogs

- Rin Tin Tin was a German shepherd trained as a police dog and left behind by retreating Germans during World War I (1914–1918). An American soldier took Rin Tin Tin home. Rin Tin Tin became a celebrity. He starred in movies. He even had his own television show.
- Mattie was a Labrador retriever that worked with police in Connecticut. In 1986, Mattie was the first dog used in fire investigations. She could sniff out evidence after a fire to help police figure out whether the fire was set on purpose.

Chapter 1

A CALL FOR HELP

The crime scene was clear of people. Copper, a brown 100-pound (45-kg) bloodhound, sniffed around an abandoned bicycle. The bike belonged to a missing boy. Copper was a police dog. He was going to help find the boy.

The call had come in to the West Valley City Police Department at approximately 5:30 p.m. It was a sunny and warm December day in Utah. A boy named Kollin had gone to play with a friend in the afternoon but had not come home for dinner. The boy's mother became worried. She called the police department for help. The police sprang into action. Along with other community members, they started to search for the missing boy.

◄ **Bloodhounds are excellent at tracking where people have gone.**

At 6:45 p.m., Sergeant Shane Matheson and his partner Copper received a call to join the search. A neighbor had found Kollin's bike on a walking path.

▲ **Police use missing people's belongings to help the dogs know what to smell for.**

▲ **Bloodhounds can follow scent trails that are several days old.**

Police officers and search members met at the site. Other teams of police dogs and their handlers were there, too.

Copper and the other dogs surrounded the bike. Their job was to pick up Kollin's scent. A police officer brought out one of Kollin's pillows to help the dogs. Copper and the other dogs sniffed the pillow. Then, with Sergeant Matheson holding tight to Copper's leash, the team set off across a field to find Kollin.

Chapter 2

TRAINING TIME

Police dogs such as Copper go through a lot of training. At a training facility, a young German shepherd snaps a white towel up in his sharp teeth. The towel is the dog's favorite toy. He wants to play tug-of-war. A handler holds the other end of the towel. The towel has been cleaned. There is no smell on it.

The game is part of the dog's police training. It is called scent work. The handler and dog play tug-of-war with the clean towel. After a rest, the handler wraps an illegal material in the towel. The towel now has a scent. The German shepherd and his handler play tug-of-war again.

◀ **Young police dogs get used to wearing harnesses and vests early in training.**

After a while, whenever the dog smells the illegal materials, he thinks of his favorite game. He follows the smell. The German shepherd learns to follow a variety of scents. The dog is not only trained to smell illegal materials. It also learns to recognize the smell of people.

Scent work is just one of the ways the puppy trains to be a police dog. The young dog does many other fun exercises. Fun is important in training because it keeps the dog from losing interest in the activity.

▲ Trainers play games with dogs in order to keep the dogs excited about the work.

▲ **Police dogs learn to stay close to their handlers in dangerous situations.**

The puppy also learns obedience. He has already learned to sit, stay, and listen to his handler's commands. The handler leads the German shepherd near a place where people fire weapons.

The weapons make loud popping noises. At first the dog is startled by each noise. He turns his head at every blast. But after spending more time at the firing range, the young dog stays calm as people shoot at targets. He stays focused on his handler.

The puppy learns **agility**, too. He completes an **obstacle** course with his handler. The dog listens to his handler's instructions. The puppy runs up a ramp and crosses a catwalk. Then he leaps over hurdles and crawls through a small tunnel. He stops and starts when he is told.

▲ **Police dogs train to become quick and sure-footed.**

▲ **Police dogs learn to stop and hold people in place with their bites.**

The police dog is also trained in bite work. A person wears a padded suit and holds a fake weapon in one hand. The person charges at the dog and handler. The young dog gets tense, but it does not move. Finally the handler tells the dog to bite. The German shepherd leaps into the air. He latches onto the arm of the person holding the fake weapon. The person cannot move.

▲ **Police departments often hold ceremonies in order to make police dogs official.**

The dog clamps down until the handler tells him to release. Then he jogs back to his handler with his tail wagging.

After many months of practice, the dog's training is complete. He takes a test to show all the things he has learned. The dog and handler pass the test. They become an official police dog team. The dog gets a lightweight **bulletproof** vest and a badge, just like the one his handler wears.

Even though the young German shepherd's training is complete, he is never done learning. The police dog and his handler continue to train every day. That way they are always ready to help when they are needed.

▲ **Police dogs and their handlers continue to learn each day on the job.**

Chapter 3

SAFE AND SOUND

Copper sniffed the ground. He pulled Sergeant Matheson forward. After 20 minutes of searching for Kollin, Copper led his handler to an open **manhole**. Someone had moved the manhole cover. There was a large circular opening in the ground.

Kollin had not seen the open manhole. He had fallen inside and was trapped! Matheson slipped into the manhole to help Kollin. He lifted the boy out of the hole and into the hands of other police officers.

Emergency workers checked Kollin for injuries. The boy had a broken elbow and some scratches. The workers brought Kollin to a hospital in the area.

◀ **Manholes lead to sewers under streets. Many manholes do not include ladders, making them difficult to enter and exit.**

▲ **Police dogs get rewarded with treats and toys after completing a case.**

Workers at the hospital put Kollin's arm in a sling. Then he was sent home with his relieved parents.

West Valley City Police told Kollin's parents that he had been trapped in the hole for three or four hours.

That amount of time would have been far longer had it not been for Copper and his keen scent work.

The following night, Kollin visited his rescuers at the police station. He rewarded Copper with a large bone! Kollin, his family, and the West Valley City Police Department were all very grateful that Kollin's story had a happy ending and that the young boy was safe. It was all thanks to Copper and his training as a police dog.

THINK ABOUT IT

- What qualities do dogs have that would help on the job as a police dog?
- What important things do a handler and a police dog learn by living and working together every day?
- Does your local police force have police dog officers? If so, how do you think they have helped your community?

GLOSSARY

agility (uh-JIL-i-tee): Agility is the ability to move quickly and easily. The dog used her agility to leap over the hurdles.

bulletproof (BUL-it-proof): Something that is bulletproof is made to stop bullets. The police officer wore a bulletproof vest.

criminals (KRIM-uh-nuhls): Criminals are people who break the law. Police dogs help catch criminals.

handler (HAND-lur): A handler is a person who trains an animal. A police dog and a handler form a team.

illegal (i-LEE-guhl): Something is illegal if it is against the law. Police dogs can smell materials that are illegal.

manhole (MAN-hole): A manhole is a covered hole in the street that leads to sewers or underground pipes. City workers enter the sewer through a manhole.

obedience (oh-BEE-dee-ens): Obedience is the act of following directions. Police dogs must learn obedience skills.

obstacle (AHB-stuh-kuhl): An obstacle is something that blocks a path. A police dog must learn how to get through an obstacle course.

retire (ri-TIRE): To retire is to stop working. Once police dogs get old enough, they retire.

TO LEARN MORE

Books

Fitzgerald, Lee. *Mounted and Canine Police*. New York: PowerKids, 2016.

Goldish, Meish. *K-9 Cops*. New York: Bearport, 2016.

Ruffin, Frances E. *Police Dogs*. New York: Bearport, 2017.

Web Sites

Visit our Web site for links about police dogs:
childsworld.com/links

Note to Parents, Teachers, and Librarians: We routinely verify our Web links to make sure they are safe and active sites. So encourage your readers to check them out!

SELECTED BIBLIOGRAPHY

Grabianowski, Ed. "How Police Dogs Work." *HowStuffWorks*. InfoSpace, 2016. Web. 2 Aug. 2016.

"K9 Dog Training: How Police Dogs Are Trained for Duty." *Puppy Institute*. Puppy Institute, 2015. Web. 2 Aug. 2016.

Manson, Pamela, and Michael McFall. "Utah Police Dog Finds Missing Boy in Manhole." *Salt Lake Tribune*. Salt Lake Tribune, 6 Dec. 2014. Web. 2 Aug. 2016.

"Police Dog I." *United States Police Canine Association Region Three*. United States Police Canine Association, n.d. Web. 2 Aug. 2016.

INDEX

ABOUT THE AUTHOR

Brandon Terrell is a writer based in Saint Paul, Minnesota. He is the author of many children's books, including picture books, chapter books, and graphic novels. When not hunched over his laptop, Brandon enjoys watching movies and television, reading, watching baseball, and spending every spare moment with his wife and their two children.